A
GREEK
TEMPLE

Series Editor	David Salariya
Book Editor	Vicki Power
Consultant	Anton Powell

Author:

Fiona Macdonald studied history at Cambridge University and at the University of East Anglia. She has taught children, adults and undergraduates. She has written many books on historical topics, mainly for children.

Illustrator:

Mark Bergin was born in Hastings in 1961. He studied at Eastbourne College of Art and specializes in historical reconstruction. He has illustrated *A World War II Submarine* and *A Medieval Castle* in the *Inside Story* series. He lives in Sussex with his wife and daughter.

Consultant:

Anton Powell has published several books about ancient Greece for children and for adult students. He has lectured for the British Museum and now teaches at the University of Wales, Cardiff. He has a special interest in reconstructing the lives and thoughts of ordinary Greek men and women.

First American edition published in 1992 by
Peter Bedrick Books
2112 Broadway
New York, NY 10023

Published in agreement with Simon & Schuster Young Books, Hemel Hempstead, England

Library of Congress Cataloging-in-Publication Data

Macdonald, Fiona.
    A Greek temple / Fiona Macdonald, Mark Bergin.
    (Inside Story)
    Includes index.
    Summary: An illustrated survey of the construction and history of the Parthenon in ancient Greece.
    ISBN 0-87226-361-4
    1. Parthenon (Athens, Greece) -- Pictorial works -- Juvenile literature. 2. Athens (Greece) -- Antiquities -- Pictorial works -- Juvenile literature. [!. Parthenon (Athens, Greece) 2. Athens (Greece -- Antiquities.] I. Bergin, Mark. II. Title. III. Series: Inside story (Peter Bedrick Books)
    DG287.P3 1992
    938'.5 -- dc20   92-10712
                                                CIP AC
Printed and bound in Hong Kong by Wing King Tong Co. Ltd.
92 93 94 95 5 4 3 2 1

INSIDE STORY

A GREEK TEMPLE

FIONA MACDONALD   MARK BERGIN

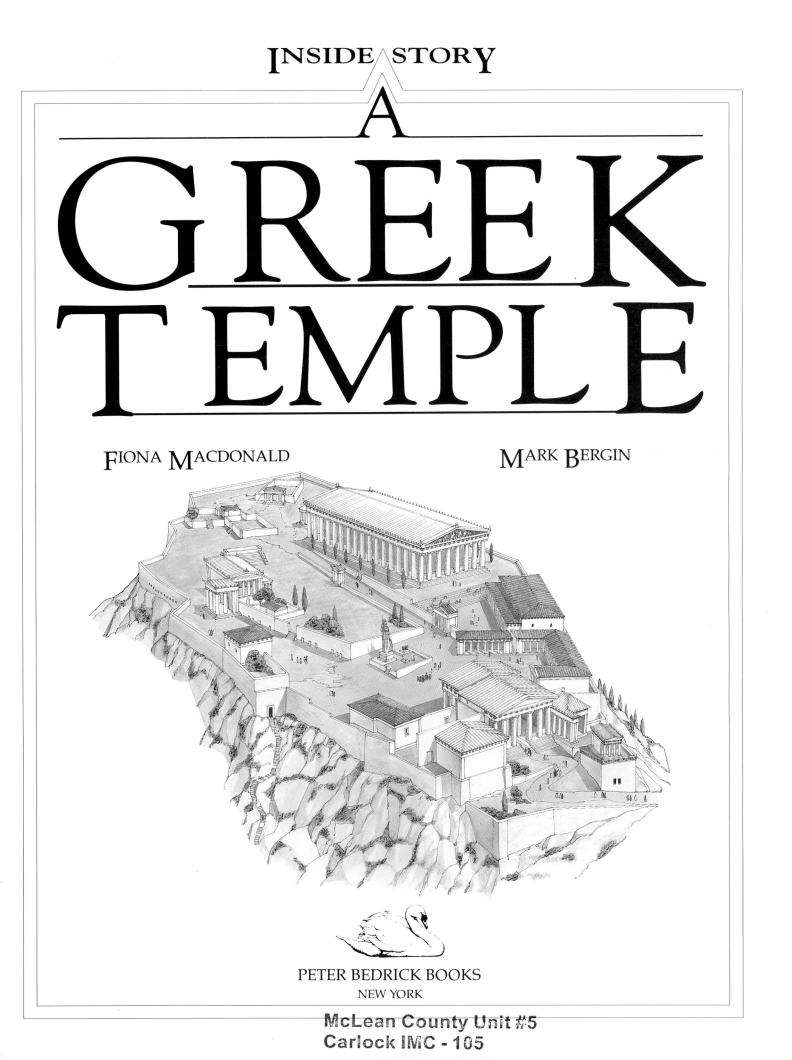

PETER BEDRICK BOOKS

NEW YORK

CONTENTS

INTRODUCTION

The Parthenon is one of the most famous buildings in the world. Many people think it is also one of the most beautiful. This book describes how it was planned and constructed, how it was decorated, and the reasons why it was built.

The Parthenon is a temple dedicated to the goddess Athena. It stands on a steep hill called the Acropolis, in the center of Athens, the capital of modern Greece. 'Acropolis' means 'high city'. In ancient times, it served as a fortress where citizens of Athens could seek refuge. The Acropolis was also a sacred site. An older temple of Athena had stood there, near a wooden statue of the goddess, who protected the city-state.

In 490 BC, Greek troops defeated the Persians at the Battle of Marathon. The Athenians decided to build a new temple on the Acropolis, to give thanks to their goddess, but this unfinished temple was destroyed by a second Persian attack in 480-79 BC. The war ended in 449 BC, and work quickly began on a new temple. It was built in honor of Athena Parthenos – Athena the Maiden. It is this temple that is known as 'the Parthenon' today.

HOMES FOR THE GODS

The earliest Greek temples were simple rooms. Their flat wooden roofs were supported on tree-trunk pillars or rough columns of stone.

Later temples were built with more elaborate pitched roofs. These were stronger, and also made the temple look more impressive.

Close-up of a temple roof. A wooden beam (called the architrave) rests on top of the pillars. Above that, crosswise rafters are covered by rows of clay tiles. The end of each rafter (known as a triglyph) is decorated. Later temples copied the same structure, but were made of stone. This was sometimes carved to look like wood.

Greek temples were built as homes for the gods. The Greeks hoped the gods would visit them there. Usually, a temple was dedicated to a single god or goddess, and housed a splendid statue, to inspire worshippers. In a big city-state, there might be several temples side by side, each marking a particular holy site. Temples had a practical use, as well. They sheltered the statues inside from birds, frost and rain.

Because they were designed as homes, early Greek temples looked like the simple, one-roomed halls in which kings and chieftains lived. Over the centuries, they became bigger and more elaborate. They were built with costly materials, and followed a strict system of design. This varied from region to region; around Athens, the Doric style was popular. Peripteral temples had a covered row of columns, called a peristyle, surrounding them.

Temples were also a way of displaying civic pride. By building a temple, a city-state could show how rich, religious and cultured it was. Temples were not cheap. It would be an insult to the citizens (and to the gods) to use shoddy materials or second-rate workmen. It took about 10 million skilled days' work to build the Parthenon.

Columns

Naos (room)

Pronaos (porch)

Pronaos (porch)

Naos

Pronaos

Row of columns

Double row of columns

Pronaos

Naos

Double row of columns

Row of columns

A 'peripteral' temple (far left). It has columns all around the naos, and a pronaos at each end.

The Parthenon (left) is a peripteral temple with a double row of columns at each end, and only one pronaos.

Athenian soldiers fighting Persian troops at the Battle of Marathon in 490 BC. The Athenian foot-soldiers, called hoplites, were outnumbered. But they fought bravely, and the Persians were driven away. Over 6,400 Persians died. The 192 Athenians killed were buried on the battlefield and honored as heroes.

A porch (left) known as a pronaos, was added to later temples. Its roof rested on columns.

Athenian warships, helped by troops from other Greek city-states, defeated more Persian invaders at the Battle of Salamis in 480 BC.

PRAYERS AND SACRIFICES

'A flourishing city honors the gods', or so one Athenian claimed. Who were these gods and goddesses? What were they like? The Greek poet Pindar described them as supermen and women. They had the same unpredictable skills and appetites as ordinary people, but on an extraordinary scale. They were 'best in strength and honor'. They lived forever, unlike men and women, who were 'creatures of a day'. And, in the words of Homer, one of the earliest Greek poets, 'There is never equality between the deathless gods and men who walk the earth.' The gods remained supreme. They controlled the destiny of all living things.

If the gods were so powerful, and men and women so weak, what was the point of worship? Could ordinary humans ever communicate with these majestic beings? The Greeks believed that it was possible, through festivals, prayers and sacrifices. They offered prayers at holy sites, or in front of statues in the temples. (They did not pray to the statues; a work of art might look godlike, but it had no powers of its own.) The Greeks offered meat, bones and blood – or other, 'pure', sacrifices, which did not involve killing – on altars built in the open air. They gave these sacrifices to the gods, hoping the gods would, in return, give blessings to them.

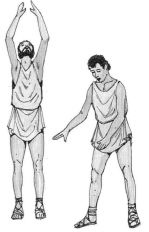

Sacrifices (left) took place on altars outside temples. Animals, birds, cakes, grain and honey were burned, while wine was sprinkled over the flames. Priests and priestesses said prayers or chanted hymns.

To pray, the Greeks raised their hands to the gods. Depending on the god they were praying to, they might face east (the direction of the rising sun) or looking out to sea.

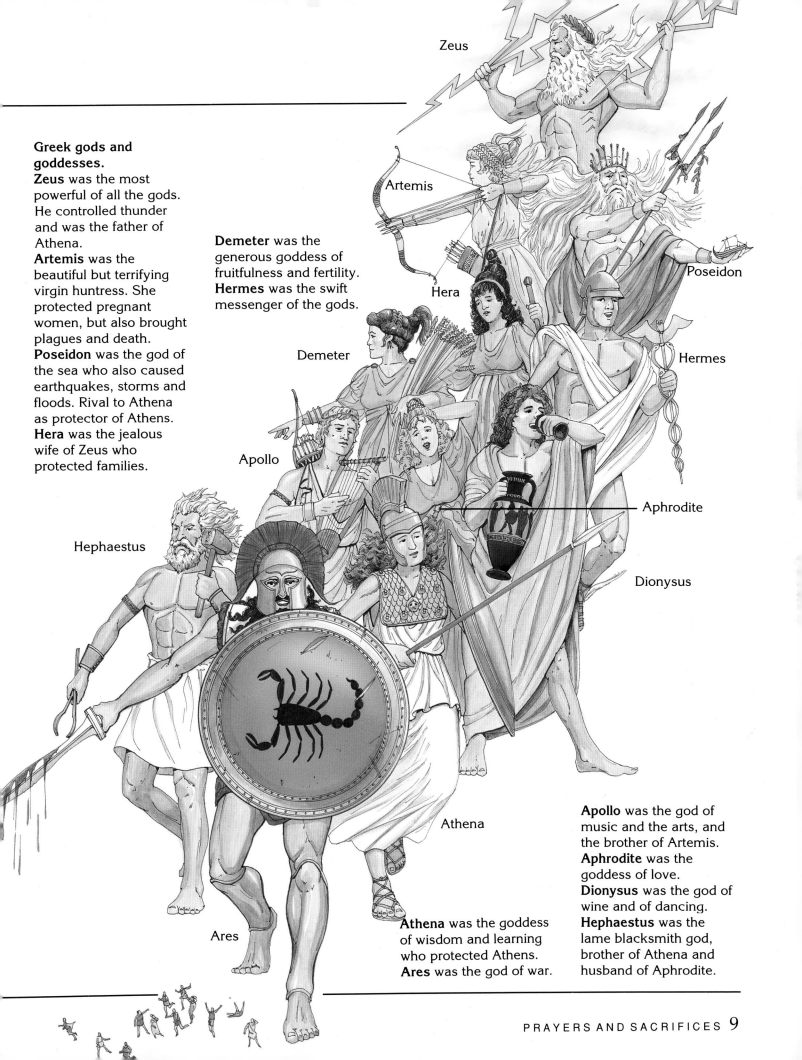

Greek gods and goddesses.
Zeus was the most powerful of all the gods. He controlled thunder and was the father of Athena.
Artemis was the beautiful but terrifying virgin huntress. She protected pregnant women, but also brought plagues and death.
Poseidon was the god of the sea who also caused earthquakes, storms and floods. Rival to Athena as protector of Athens.
Hera was the jealous wife of Zeus who protected families.

Demeter was the generous goddess of fruitfulness and fertility.
Hermes was the swift messenger of the gods.

Zeus

Artemis

Hera

Demeter

Poseidon

Hermes

Apollo

Aphrodite

Hephaestus

Dionysus

Athena

Ares

Apollo was the god of music and the arts, and the brother of Artemis.
Aphrodite was the goddess of love.
Dionysus was the god of wine and of dancing.
Hephaestus was the lame blacksmith god, brother of Athena and husband of Aphrodite.

Athena was the goddess of wisdom and learning who protected Athens.
Ares was the god of war.

FESTIVAL GAMES

The great sanctuary (temple and surrounding buildings) dedicated to the god Apollo at Delphi in central Greece.

Sick people came to Delphi to sleep in hospitals near the temple. They hoped Apollo might visit and cure them.

The oracle was drugged by inhaling smoke from burning laurel leaves. Priests repeated her answers and explained what they meant.

Today, we do not associate sports with religion. But, for the Greeks, sporting competitions were one of the best ways of pleasing their gods. Because they believed that gods and goddesses were, in many ways, similar to humans, it seemed safe to assume they would enjoy the same pleasures. Festival games took place close to many temples, and were held on holy days throughout the year. These holy days were also 'holidays' – as if the Superbowl were combined with Christmas Day. There was all the excitement of watching sports, singing festival hymns, eating roast meat from sacrifices and getting time off work.

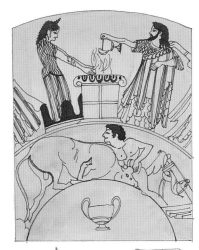

Two illustrations of religious sacrifices from painted pottery, made in Athens around 500 BC. The top picture shows a pig being sacrificed on a god's altar. Meat was a luxury in Greece, and so it was a fitting gift to offer to a god or goddess. But the Greeks did not burn the entire animal. They offered the god the entrails and bones, but cooked and ate the rest of the meat themselves.

The lower picture shows a priestess supervising a sacrificial fire, while a worshipper pours on wine from a fine vase.

Victory in the games was a blessing from the gods. It was one way of knowing they were pleased – with certain competitors, at least. But some sportsmen were not content to leave the results of their races in the hands of the gods. Cheating was quite common among sportsmen, so Greek referees always carried a big stick.

The will of the gods could be discovered in other ways. At Delphi, for example, a priestess acted as 'oracle'; she lost control of her own thoughts and spoke with the voice of Apollo. Worshippers asked questions like, 'Should our troops go to war?' or, more personally, 'Should I leave my wife?'

The great temple and its surrounding sports center at Olympia. The first Olympic games were held in 776 BC.

Athletes and spectators stayed in well-designed buildings. There were hostels, training tracks, baths and a stadium.

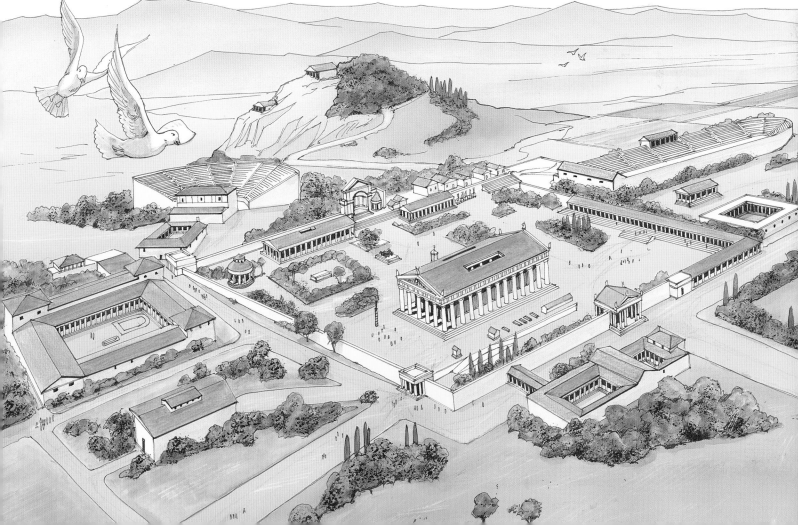

TEMPLE DESIGN

The Greeks first settled in their homeland before 1600 BC. By the 5th century BC they had become strong, confident and prosperous. They won the admiration and respect of peoples living nearby. At times, the Greek city-states fought bitterly among themselves, but, as the Persian invasions of 490-479 BC had shown, their country was still a rich prize to tempt a would-be conqueror.

   The Greeks' achievements were reflected in their art. It, too, was confident and strong. Buildings and sculptures dating from the 5th century BC, especially those made in Athens, are often described as 'classical'. That is, they are calm, well-made, and designed within the limits of good taste and traditional style. There are no jarring special effects, no gimmicks, and no attempts to surprise or startle with 'the shock of the new'.

The Treasury of the Athenians, Delphi, c. 500 BC. It is similar to earlier temples: a room and porch (pronaos), but made of stone.

A porch could be added at each end of a temple, for decoration rather than use, like at the Temple of Nike in Athens, built c. 420 BC.

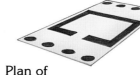

Plan of
Temple of Nike

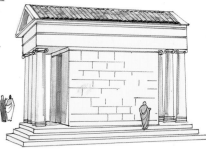

By around 447 BC, when work on the Parthenon was started, Greek temples were becoming larger, although the plan and decoration remained simple. This is a temple dedicated to Hephaestus (left), built in Athens in the 5th century BC.

Plan of
Hephaestion

A temple (below) built in Ionia, Turkey. It was planned and decorated in a more elaborate style.

Plan of
Ionic
temple

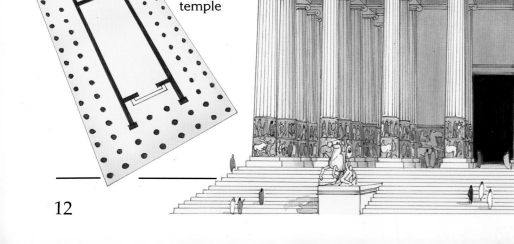

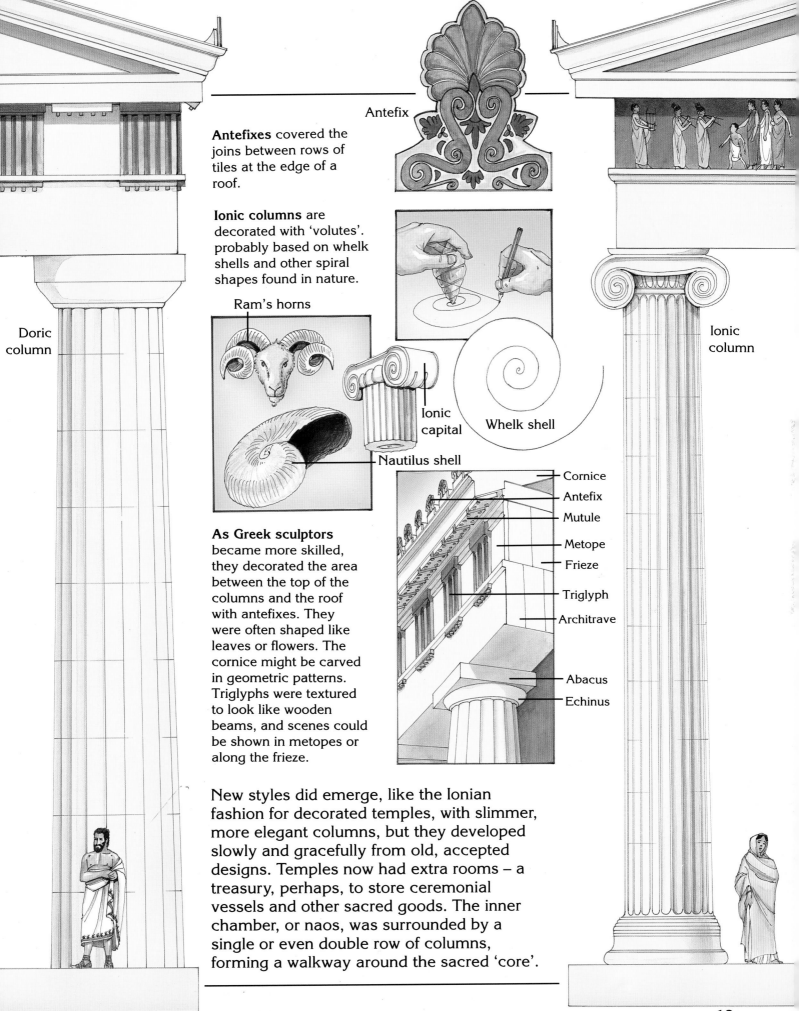

Antefixes covered the joins between rows of tiles at the edge of a roof.

Antefix

Ionic columns are decorated with 'volutes'. probably based on whelk shells and other spiral shapes found in nature.

Ram's horns

Doric column

Ionic capital

Nautilus shell

Whelk shell

Ionic column

As Greek sculptors became more skilled, they decorated the area between the top of the columns and the roof with antefixes. They were often shaped like leaves or flowers. The cornice might be carved in geometric patterns. Triglyphs were textured to look like wooden beams, and scenes could be shown in metopes or along the frieze.

Cornice
Antefix
Mutule
Metope
Frieze
Triglyph
Architrave
Abacus
Echinus

New styles did emerge, like the Ionian fashion for decorated temples, with slimmer, more elegant columns, but they developed slowly and gracefully from old, accepted designs. Temples now had extra rooms – a treasury, perhaps, to store ceremonial vessels and other sacred goods. The inner chamber, or naos, was surrounded by a single or even double row of columns, forming a walkway around the sacred 'core'.

PERFECT PROPORTIONS

Almost as soon as it was built, the Parthenon was recognised as a triumph of Greek classical style. The scholar Plutarch, writing 500 years after the Parthenon was built but using contemporary documents, describes the onlookers' feelings: 'The buildings rose, matchless in beauty and grace, while the workers vied with one another in the skill of their craftsmanship.'

The Parthenon is a very big building – it is almost 230 feet long and over 100 feet wide – yet it appears delicate, poised and serene. It is 'matchless' and successful because of its proportions. It is wider than Doric temples usually were; there are eight columns along the front, not six. It seems that the Parthenon's architects worked out a subtle mathematical pattern as the basis for their design. The ratios – or relationship – between the temple's height and its width and its length and its width are both 9:4. There is the same mathematical relationship between the distance from one column to another and each column's diameter. Amazingly, our eyes can take in and appreciate this mathematical harmony without understanding any of the measurements involved.

The Parthenon as it might have appeared around 438 BC, the year it was completed. It made a fitting home for the great gold and ivory statue of Athena.

The Parthenon.
1. East front.
2. Double row of columns forming the pronaos (porch).
3. Metopes.
4. Frieze.
5. Pediment with sculpture.
6. Peristyle. (Single row of columns along side of temple.)
7. Base (platform).
8. East doorway.
9. Naos (room).
10. Chryselephantine (gold and ivory) statue of Athena.
11. Two tiers of slender columns to support roof.
12. Decoration of garlands (leaves and fine cloth).
13. Architrave.
14. Frieze.
15. Tiled roof (made of thin slices of marble).
16. Wooden roof beam.
17. Wooden rafter.
18. Antefix.
19. Acroterion (decoration on roof).
20. Back room (used as a treasury).

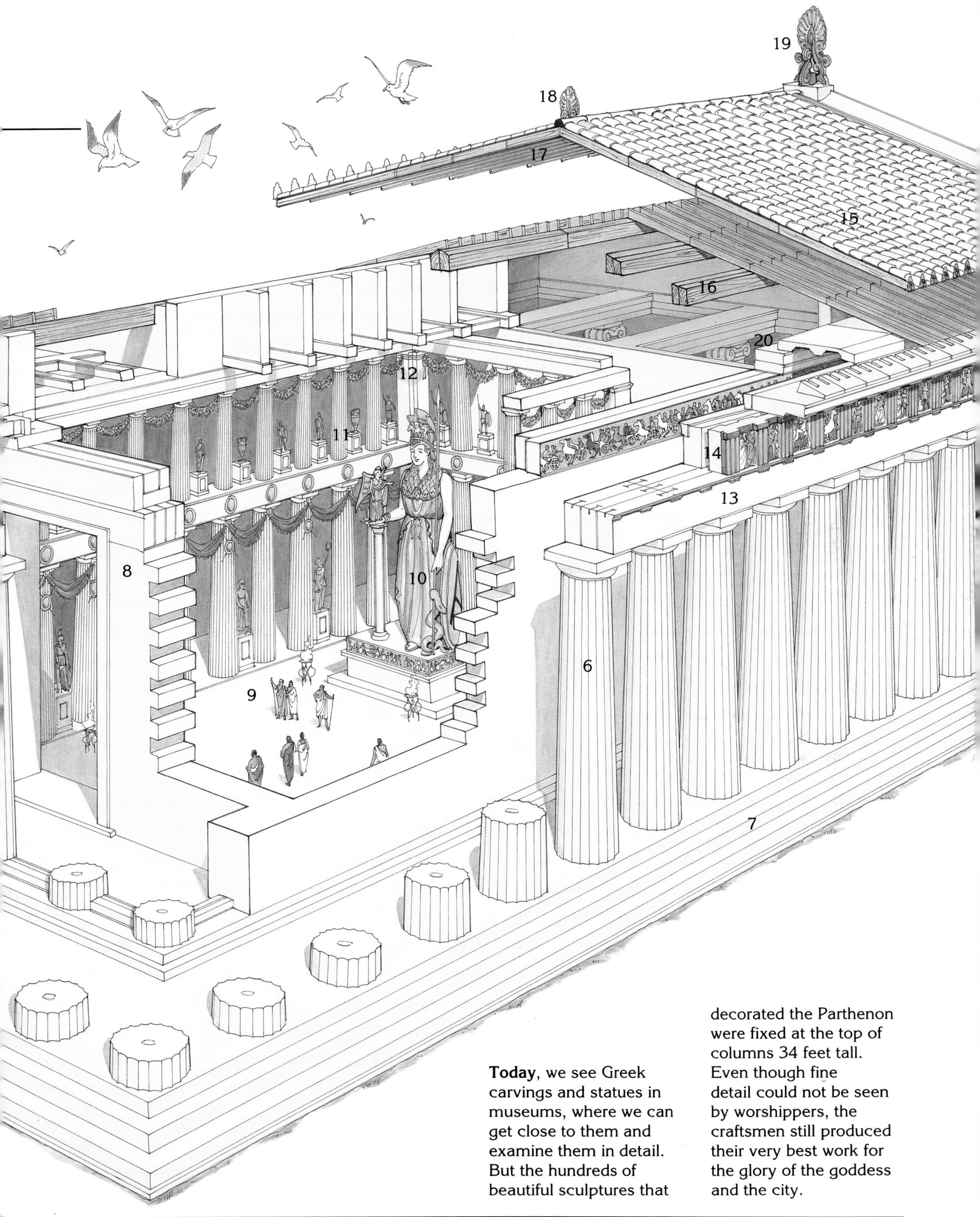

19

18

17

15

16

20

12

11

14

13

8

10

9

6

7

Today, we see Greek carvings and statues in museums, where we can get close to them and examine them in detail. But the hundreds of beautiful sculptures that decorated the Parthenon were fixed at the top of columns 34 feet tall. Even though fine detail could not be seen by worshippers, the craftsmen still produced their very best work for the glory of the goddess and the city.

PREPARING THE SITE

Erechtheum temple   Site of old temple of Athena

Wall

The main Greek city-states (above). After 480 BC, Athens controlled many weaker city-states in southern Greece.

Marble for the Parthenon (below) came from Mount Pentelikon, 10 miles from Athens.

The Acropolis was not an easy place to build a large temple. The ground was hard and rocky, with a thin, gritty soil. Parts of the site sloped steeply, especially to the south. The builders had to construct a huge buttress wall to support the platform on which the Parthenon would stand. Work on this had started soon after the Battle of Marathon in 490 BC, but the Parthenon's builders had to extend these earlier foundations, to provide for their temple and its new, more perfect, design. Although the foundations were made from limestone, a common building stone in Greece, the rest of the Parthenon was built of marble, which gleams and glistens in the bright Greek sun.

Wooden wedges were hammered into marble. Water was poured on top. The wood swelled, cracking the marble.

The corners were then cut off the rough blocks, leaving four projecting lugs to use for lifting.

Blocks of marble were cut by chipping grooves in the solid rock face using mallets and chisels. Architects gave instructions for precise block sizes and shapes.

The rough drum-shaped sections were neatened and checked. Then they were ready to carry to the building site.

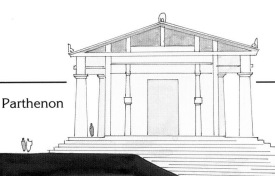

Parthenon

Rain water cistern

Foundations

Rubble, earth and earlier walls

Buttress wall

Cross section through the Acropolis (left), the hill that formed the 'heart' of Athens. Important civic and religious buildings stood there. The foundations for the Parthenon were deep and strong because the hilltop site falls steeply away on the southern side.

The Parthenon appears to be made of straight lines. But in fact, almost everything about it is curved. This is not accidental. The architects who designed it knew that our eyes sometimes play tricks. They had to plan a building that looked straight, even if, when measured, that straightness turned out to be an illusion. They also knew that slight irregularity makes a building look 'alive'. By careful measurement, we can see how these 'architectural refinements' work. All the pillars bulge slightly, and are set at an almost imperceptible angle. The steps, the pediment and the roof itself are all gently curved.

The foundations of the Parthenon were built on the base of an earlier temple, planned to commemorate soldiers killed at the Battle of Marathon.

Cave with sacred spring

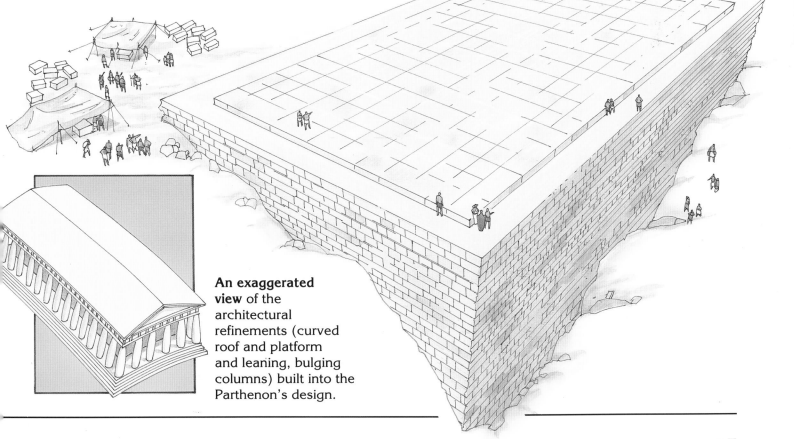

An exaggerated view of the architectural refinements (curved roof and platform and leaning, bulging columns) built into the Parthenon's design.

CITIZENS AND WORKERS

The two architects of the Parthenon (below) – Iktinos and Kallikrates.

Pheidias, the sculptor chosen to make the statue of Athena and to supervise other carvers.

The citizens of Athens sent representatives to the Assembly, a meeting to decide on the city's plans and policies.

Only free Athenians could take part in the Assembly. Foreigners, women and slaves were not entitled to vote.

Athens was a democracy. This meant that all adult male citizens had a right to air their views on any major enterprise involving the city-state and its wealth. There were long discussions before the decision to build the Parthenon was made. It was just one of several important building projects (including walls and a concert hall) started at this time.

They were planned by the Athenian statesman Pericles (c. 494-429 BC), partly to add glory to the city-state, and partly to provide work for the soldiers that were unemployed now the Persian wars were over. It seems strange to think that one of the greatest buildings in the western world was planned as part of a job-creation scheme.

Painters decorated the finished carvings with touches of bright color.

Dyers used expensive herbs, earth and shells to dye Athena's robe.

The leathercutter made shoes for the workmen.

Young girls embroidered the edges of Athena's 'peplos', or long robe.

Above
Sailors and merchants brought gold, ivory and other precious goods from overseas.

Below
Waggon-drivers led heavily-laden ox-carts from the marble quarries to the building site.

The site foremen and overseers. They controlled craftsmen and gangs of workmen.

Carpenters made hoists, scaffolding and rafters to support the roof.

Stonemasons carved the costly white marble into columns and blocks.

Coppersmiths made metal ornaments for the statues used to decorate the Parthenon.

Unskilled laborers, including the unemployed soldiers, made a good start on the Parthenon site, leveling the ground, checking the marble blocks that had been carried there to build the earlier, uncompleted temple, and helping to drag fresh loads of stone up the steep Acropolis slopes.

Skilled laborers carried out the rest of the work, and were paid at the same rate as the men who supervised the project. It has been suggested that the supervisors were wealthy and well-educated Athenians who performed this task as a service to their city-state, and not for any financial reward.

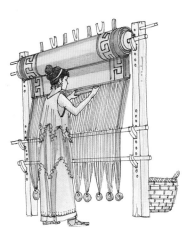

Roadbuilders toiled in the hot sun to make paths for men, mules and ox-carts.

Skilled craftsmen prepared thin layers of ivory and gold leaf ready for use in Athena's statue.

Weavers made clothes for the workmen, and a fine robe for Athena.

Modelmakers helped plan the Parthenon's layout and design.

Ropemakers twisted strong ropes to help lift heavy blocks of building stone into place.

COLUMNS AND WALLS

Once the foundations for the Parthenon were in place, the base of the temple could be built. This was a wide platform, edged by finely-chiseled steps. The top step, called the stylobate, was later smoothed and polished. Its white surface would help illuminate the temple with softly-reflected light. It was a difficult task to raise the columns; each was made of 8 or 10 sections, which had to be cut to shape on the ground, then heaved into position using ropes, pulleys and cranes.

Ramps and slipways were used to move heavy blocks of marble. Some of these slipways survive, and can still be seen on the Acropolis. Hauling stone was hard work for men and animals. The Athenians rewarded mules who worked well by setting them free, allowing them to wander all over the city-state, grazing when and where they chose.

Finished blocks of stone were eased into place using sticks and levers. The builders did not use cement. Instead, each block was joined to the neighboring one with 'double T' strips of iron. Every strip was coated in lead to make sure that it would not crumble away. If this happened, the wall would crack and collapse.

The inner walls of the Parthenon were made of squared-off blocks of marble finished with a technique called anathyrosis. The ends of each block were hollowed in the middle, leaving an outer border, like a picture-frame, where each block touched. This helped masons achieve a close fit when the blocks were levered in, side by side.

Oxen, mules and men were used to cart the blocks of marble from the quarry, and to haul them up the steep slopes of the Acropolis. Stone was not transported in winter, because the roads were too muddy. Once the rough-cut stones had reached the building site, they were carefully trimmed into shape by skilled stonemasons. Men came to Athens from all over Greece, eager to find work.

Craftsmen used simple tools, mostly made of iron, including picks (1 and 2), chisels (3), punches (4) and drills (5). They held the tips of these against the stone with in one hand, while striking the ends with wooden hammers and mallets (6).

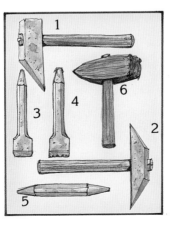

THE TEMPLE ROOF

The roof tiles of the Parthenon were cut from high-quality Parian marble, which was normally used for statues. Its fine grain allowed it to be sliced into thin sections; the tiles were only about 1 inch thick. Some historians have suggested that they were cut so thin to let light into the temple – marble is slightly translucent. But others argue that this would not have worked. They think the architects' main concern was to stop the roof becoming so heavy that it bowed the columns and cracked the walls.

The architects' thoroughness is also revealed by the position of the antefixes. Normally, these were placed at the end of each row of cover tiles. But, since the marble tiles were small, with many covered joins, that would have resulted in too many antefixes, making the roof look fussy and cluttered. The architects therefore placed them between alternate rows of tiles, where they would create the best visual effect.

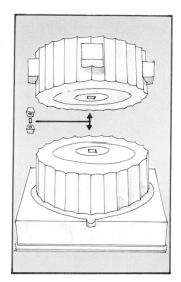

The surface of each column block was carefully prepared. An outer 'ring' was trimmed smooth, ready for finishing. The next ring was left rough, to grip. The center was fitted with a bung, which held the blocks together.

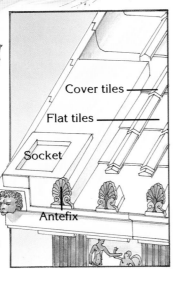

Cover tiles

Flat tiles

Socket

Antefix

Once the column blocks had been hauled into place, the rough outer lugs were chiseled off and the column was ready for smoothing and fluting. Cutting flutes was an extremely skilled task. Each groove had to be perfectly straight, and aligned with all the other flutes. The slightest error could ruin the appearance of the whole temple.

1. Rough area removed.
2. Trimmed to shape.
3. Rough grooves cut.
4. Flutes shaped.

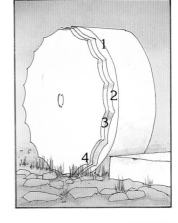

Temple roofs (above and right) were made of wooden rafters, covered with thin wood strips called battens, and then a layer of tiles. These were usually 'pantiles' made of fired clay, but the tiles of the Parthenon were made from imported marble. Two sorts of tile were used: flat tiles, with curving edges and ridges underneath (so they could sit on the battens) and cover tiles, which covered the joins between rows of flat tiles.

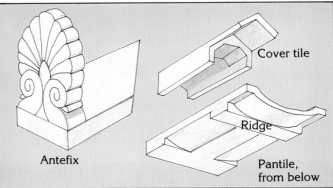

Antefix

Cover tile

Ridge

Pantile, from below

The 'boundary' between the roof and the sky was marked by acroteria. These were free-standing sculptures slotted into holes at key points on the roof. In contrast to the clean lines of the pillars, the acroteria were carved in flowing, plant-based designs.

PARTHENON SCULPTURES

Acroterion

West Pediment

The West Pediment shows Athena winning the contest to watch over Athens. Athenian citizens liked to feel they were the best in Greece, and specially favored by the gods.

Many Doric temples had some carved decoration, and Ionic temples had even more. But the Parthenon was unique in both the quantity and high quality of the sculptures that were used to decorate its outer 'face'. These sculptures were placed in three important locations – the pediments, the metopes and the frieze.

The sculptures on the pediments were the last to be carved (between 438-432 BC) but they were almost certainly the first to be seen by anyone approaching the Parthenon from the city-state of Athens. Their sheer size caught the attention – all 50 figures on the pediment were far larger than life.

The pediment sculptures, which show gods and goddesses, were carved 'in the round'; the back of each figure was properly finished, even though no-one on the ground could see it. Only fragments of these sculptures survive today, but drawings made in 1674 show us what they looked like. The center panel of the East Pediment – the one people saw first – portrayed a myth that was important to Athenians. It showed how their patron goddess, Athena, was born fully-grown from the head of Zeus. The West Pediment showed how the god Poseidon challenged Athena for the right to protect Athens. There are more myths about Athena on page 45.

Metal bars (left) were used to tie the Parthenon building blocks together.

Wooden scaffolding was built to aid workers. Finished sections of sculpture were hauled up to the pediment using strong ropes.

East Pediment

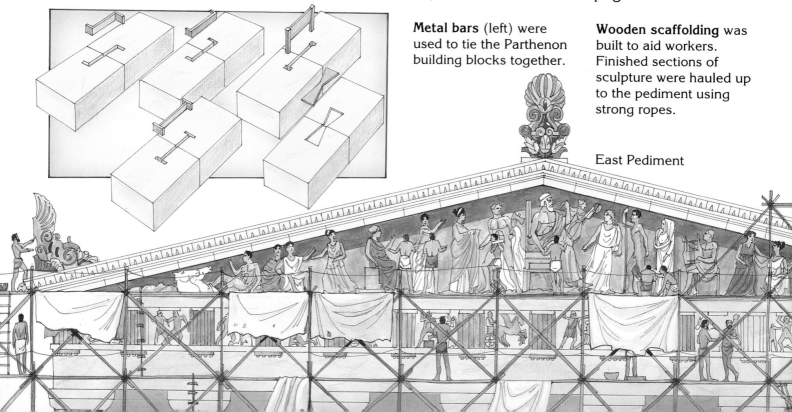

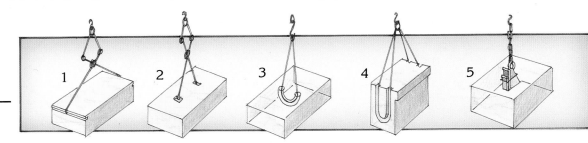

Methods of hoisting
stone using tongs (1, 2)
and rope (3, 4, 5).

**The Parthenon's
sculptures** had to be
carefully designed to fit
into difficult spaces. The
East and West
Pediments were shaped
like long flat triangles,
with narrow sections at
each end. For the West
Pediment (above) the
sculptors cleverly
decided to fill this area
with carvings of river-
gods and sea-gods, lying
down or emerging from
the water. On the East
Pediment (below), they
showed just the heads of
the horses that
(according to Greek
myths) pull the moon-
goddess in her chariot
across the night sky, first
rising slowly into view,
then sinking beneath the
horizon towards the
break of day.

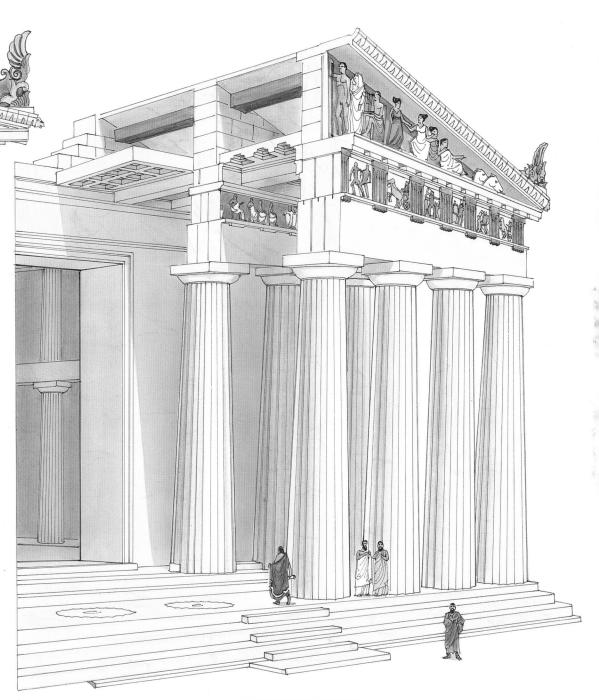

Left
The frieze as visitors to
the Parthenon would
have seen it, high above
the columns on the north
side of the temple.

THE CRAFTSMAN'S DAY

6 am Sunrise – it is summertime. Gets up, puts on cloak, washes hands and face.

6:30 am Has breakfast – bread, olives, figs or grapes, and wine mixed with a lot of water.

7:00 am Walks to building site. Sees merchants and market traders at work.

8:00 am Discusses the day's work with the foreman, who gives orders to all the workers.

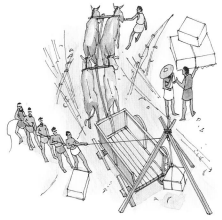

9:00 am Helps unload blocks of stone that came from quarry. Talks to mule driver about conditions on the roads.

11:00 am Keeps lookout on scaffolding while work mates haul up drum-shaped block to be added to a column.

12 noon Eats lunch in the shade – bread, cheese, onions. Drinks lots of water; the building site is hot.

3:00 pm Admires work of craftsmen who are fluting columns. Rushes to help as roof-worker accidentally falls.

4:00 pm Meets with senior politicians and priests who visit the site to check on the progress of work.

6:00 pm At sports center for a rub-down with oil to wash away dirt and dust. On his way out, watches a wrestling match.

8:00 pm Dinner with family – bread, bean stew with garlic, fruit and cheese. Wine mixed with water to drink.

9:00 pm Neighbor calls. Wife and children go to bed. Men discuss politics and sports. Slave brings wine and cakes.

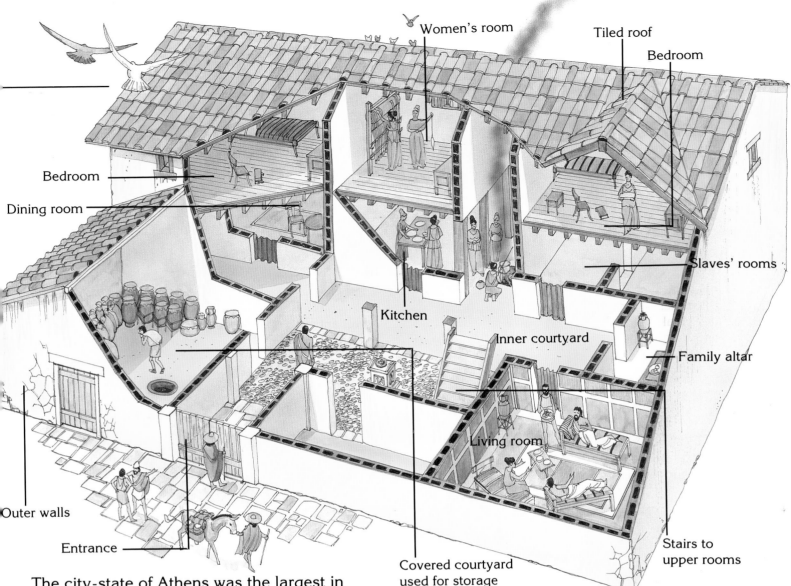

Women's room

Tiled roof

Bedroom

Bedroom

Dining room

Slaves' rooms

Kitchen

Inner courtyard

Family altar

Living room

Outer walls

Entrance

Stairs to upper rooms

Covered courtyard used for storage

The city-state of Athens was the largest in ancient Greece, if measured by population, rather than area. In the mid-5th century BC, about 60,000 adult men lived there. The total population, including women, children, slaves and resident foreigners (called metics) would make perhaps 350,000 people in all.

Most of these people worked hard to earn their living. A few wealthy nobles lived off the profits of their estates, but ordinary people worked as merchants, sailors, potters, builders, market traders and entertainers. Women and slaves worked to make homes comfortable. Sculptors and stonemasons settled there temporarily, then moved away to work on another new temple elsewhere. Athens also attracted people who lived by their brains. It was the home of philosophers, teachers, dramatists, mathematicians and priests. As Pericles said, Athens was 'an education to the rest of Greece'.

House belonging to a wealthy Greek family, perhaps of a politician or priest.

Workers lived in smaller houses with fewer rooms, but built to a similar plan.

Athenian intellectuals prized excellence in everything, and the Athenian government encouraged fair treatment for all its citizens. A good craftsman, like one of the sculptors working on the Parthenon, could expect – and get – respect. People did not look down on him because he worked with his hands. It was a common joke that you could not tell rich Athenians from their slaves. Most people wore simple clothes, lived in mud-brick houses, ate plain food, and surrounded themselves with as many beautiful objects as they could afford to buy.

INSIDE THE PARTHENON

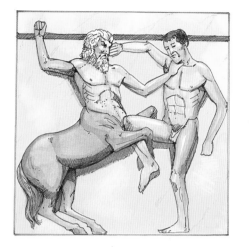

Two metopes (left) showing a Greek myth. Greek tribesmen, called Lapiths, are fighting centaurs (a centaur is half-man, half horse). In the myth, the Lapiths won the battle. The architects chose to decorate the Parthenon with this myth because it showed the triumph of Greek civilization over crudeness and brutality.

After admiring the carvings on the metopes and frieze, and, perhaps, thinking about what they meant, visitors entering the Parthenon would need a few moments for their eyes to adjust to the darkness within. For a little while it would feel like stepping into another world – a holy world, wreathed in incense and echoing with chanted hymns. In the dark, they could see a mighty figure: the goddess Athena. Her ivory flesh shone softly, her golden robe glowed, and her eyes glittered with the cold fire of jewels. Her waist and wrists were wreathed with snakes, and, like a monstrous brooch, she wore a severed head upon her breast.

That is one way of thinking about the statue of Athena, over 39 feet tall, that stood in the naos of the Parthenon. Some Athenians may have experienced it like that. But others would simply have admired it as a fine work of art, or as a rich gift to their goddess. Athena's statue was a wooden frame, covered with plates of ivory and gold. It was designed by Pheidias, the best sculptor in Greece. He was criticized for including portraits of himself and his patron, Pericles, on Athena's shield. Sadly, his great work is lost, but we know what it looked like from copies made in Roman times, and from reports of travelers who saw it.

Right
Carving and painting the frieze. The Parthenon was completed in only 10 years, between 447 and 438 BC. The panels making up the frieze were carved between 442 and 438 BC. A great many skilled craftsmen must have worked to produce this huge piece of sculpture in so short a time. They were trained and guided by Pheidias, the great sculptor who made the gold and ivory statue of the goddess Athena.

The metopes (above) were made between 447-442 BC. The frieze was carved later. By this time, the sculptors had grown more skilful.

The carvings on the frieze are of much higher quality, and in one style. The sculptors had learned how to work well together.

Right
The huge statue of Athena, in place inside the Parthenon, towers over mortal men.

THE ACROPOLIS

Buildings on the Acropolis as they would have looked during the late 5th century BC, at the height of Athens' power and fame.

1. Arrephorion – home of the young girls who wove the peplos robe offered every year to Athena.
2. Pandroseion – tomb of an ancient hero-king.
3. Erechtheum – a small temple dedicated to Athena and to Poseidon.
4. Altar of Athena – site of the earliest temple dedicated to the goddess and the holiest place on the Acropolis.

Erechtheum

The Parthenon towers over all other buildings on the Acropolis, just as the Acropolis towers above Athens. Yet it is only one of several remarkable temples and buildings that stand on the 'high city'. They were all constructed after 480 BC to replace earlier holy buildings destroyed in the Persian attack.

This great rebuilding program did not go ahead unopposed. Thucydides, an Athenian politician, argued that it was wrong to 'deck our city like a vain woman with precious stones and statues and thousand-talent [a huge sum] temples'. But he was overruled, and in 447 BC building work began. First came the Parthenon, then the Propylaia, then the Nike temple, then the Erechtheum (started in 420 BC). Other, smaller, buildings followed soon after.

Caryatid (column in the shape of a woman) from the Erechtheum.

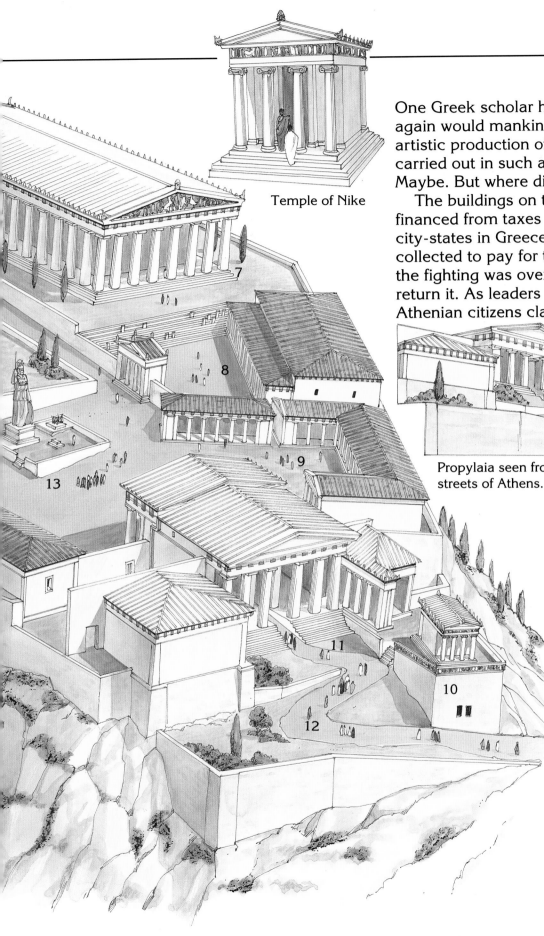

Temple of Nike

One Greek scholar has said, 'Perhaps never again would mankind see such concentrated artistic production of such high quality carried out in such a short space of time.' Maybe. But where did the money come from?

The buildings on the Acropolis were financed from taxes sent by smaller, weaker city-states in Greece. The money had been collected to pay for the Persian wars. But now the fighting was over, Athens refused to return it. As leaders of the Greek defence, Athenian citizens claimed it as their reward.

Propylaia seen from streets of Athens.

5. Sanctuary of Zeus Polieus, where worshippers sacrificed oxen.
6. Sanctuary of Pandion, an ancient hero-king.
7. The Parthenon.
8. Chalkotheke (where holy objects and offerings were kept.)
9. Bruaroneion (sanctuary of Artemis).
10. Temple of Nike (goddess of victory).
11. Propylaia (grand gateway).
12. Approach path and steps.
13. Statue of Athena Promachos – a colossal bronze statue showing the goddess in full armor. Her spear-tip served as a beacon to sailors entering harbor.

ATHENA'S BIRTHDAY

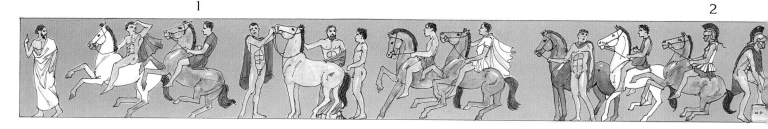

1   2

The West Frieze.
For the first time ever in Greece, the architects of the Parthenon decided to decorate a temple with scenes from everyday life. They chose the citizens of Athens taking part in the procession of the Great Panathenaia as their subject. Here are groups of young men and their horses, preparing to join in the procession and take part in the festival games. They are shown in a variety of ways:

(1) Cantering towards the procession's starting point at the Diplyon (double) Gate, close to the Kerameikos quarter of the city, where the potters worked; (2) wearing plumed helmets and putting on armor;

(3) dressed in the cloaks and shady hats worn by travelers; (4) having trouble controlling their excited mounts and (5) naked, except for a short tunic (this was for artistic effect; the Greeks did not ride in the nude).

Visitors to Athens remarked that the city had more holidays than anywhere else in Greece. This was true. Festivals took place regularly throughout the year. The most important was in honor of the goddess Athena. It was celebrated every summer (in the Athenian New Year) and was called the Panathenaia. Even more magnificent was the Great Panathenaia, a special version of the yearly Panathenaia festival, held every fourth year. It included sports and games, besides the music, dancing and sacrifices that took place every year.

The Athenians thought of the Panathenaia as Athena's birthday. So, naturally, they gave her a present. For as long as anyone could remember, this had been a new dress (or 'peplos') traditionally woven in yellow and blue. The peplos was carried through the city-state on a cart shaped like a ship, followed by a grand festival procession. On the slopes of the Acropolis the peplos was unloaded, and carried on foot to drape the ancient wooden statue of the goddess that stood on the summit. Once the Parthenon was built, the procession extended its route to pass alongside the new temple. Appropriately, Pheidias's gold and ivory statue of Athena was dedicated at the Great Panathenaia of 438 BC.

3

The soldiers shown on the frieze delivered a political message. They portrayed warfare as glorious. That is why the sculptors carved only handsome men. For the Greeks, physical beauty reflected a noble character inside. This message was necessary because there had been disagreements between the city leaders and citizens about the high costs of war.

4

5

THE GREAT FESTIVAL

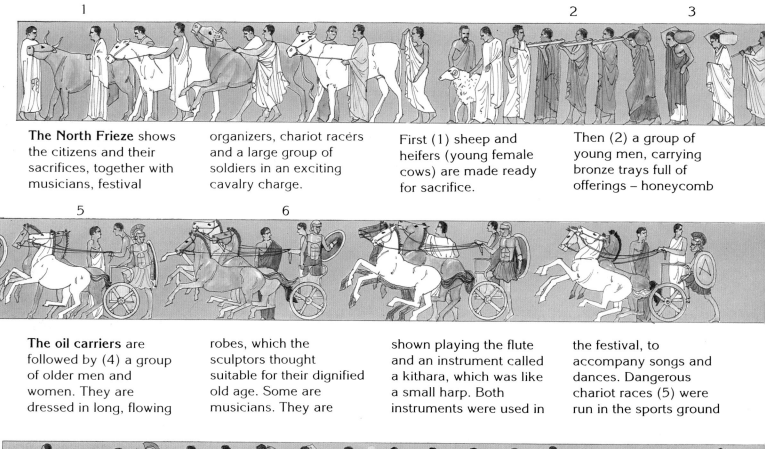

The North Frieze shows the citizens and their sacrifices, together with musicians, festival

organizers, chariot racers and a large group of soldiers in an exciting cavalry charge.

First (1) sheep and heifers (young female cows) are made ready for sacrifice.

Then (2) a group of young men, carrying bronze trays full of offerings – honeycomb

The oil carriers are followed by (4) a group of older men and women. They are dressed in long, flowing

robes, which the sculptors thought suitable for their dignified old age. Some are musicians. They are

shown playing the flute and an instrument called a kithara, which was like a small harp. Both instruments were used in

the festival, to accompany songs and dances. Dangerous chariot races (5) were run in the sports ground

The Panathenaia started with an all-night vigil on the Acropolis. Young men and girls sang and danced by starlight in honor of the goddess. Then, at daybreak, the procession began. The flame on Athena's altar, where animal offerings were burnt, was lit by the winner of a race between runners carrying flaming torches. Then the heavy 'ship' carrying the peplos lumbered through the city and across the marketplace on its way towards Athena's statue. Citizens not chosen to take part watched from the roadside. The crowds could be enormous; one wealthy noble was mocked for building a special stand so his girlfriend could get a good view.

Celebrations at the four-yearly Great Panathenaia were the same, but with the addition of games (first introduced to Athens in 566 BC), and a music festival at another of Pericles's new Athenian buildings: the Odeion. Rich prizes were offered at all these events. As well as the famous Athenian olive oil, there was money, food and 'crowns' made of wild olive branches trimmed with gold. Festival sports included running, boxing, pentathlon, wrestling, horse and chariot races, javelin-throwing, war-dancing and a regatta. Teams competed for a prize in all-around strength and fitness, known to the Greeks as 'Manly Excellence'.

4

and cakes – to give to the goddess. Other young men (3) carry jars of precious olive oil;

myths told how Athena first gave olive trees to the Athenians. Beautifully-decorated

jars of oil, made in Athens and showing pictures of the goddess on one side, and

sportsmen on the other, were offered as prizes in the Great Panathenaic festival games.

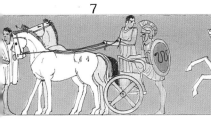

7

outside Athens' city walls. The clothes and armor worn by the charioteers and their passengers vary quite

widely in style (see, for example, 6 and 7). It is as if the sculptors were in too great a hurry to worry about precise

details. This variety of styles suggests that there were many different sculptors at work on this section of the frieze.

Each sculptor has probably carved the weapons and clothing typical of his own home city.

MEMORIAL

1

The panels on the South Frieze reflect the Athenians' recent experience of war, and the way in which military activities had become incorporated in the Great Panathenaic procession. At (1) are 'apobatai'. These fully armed soldiers performed a brave and dangerous display. They jumped on and off the swiftly-moving chariots, somehow managing to

Following the chariots are a group of elderly citizens (2). Although the Parthenon's sculptors set out to portray the festival procession, their version of it on the frieze is hardly true to life. From other evidence – city records, treasurer's accounts, inscriptions and travelers' tales, we know that many groups of citizens and even the metics (foreigners, who are shown on the friezes wearing red cloaks to distinguish them from 'real' Athenians) joined in. Yet few ordinary

Some historians suggest there was a somber message contained in the Parthenon's friezes: that they were designed as a memorial to the Athenian soldiers who were killed at Marathon. The dead men were buried on the battlefield. The Athenians planned to commemorate them in an earlier temple, but, as described on page 5, that had been destroyed. This theory would explain why there are 192 men shown in the Parthenon's frieze, exactly the number who died at Marathon. It would also explain why the sculptors filled their work with images of soldiers, rather than recording all the other participants in the great procession.

Whatever its message, the Parthenon frieze has always been admired, because the sculptors used subtle devices to perfect their work. For example, the stone at the top of each panel is over 2 inches thicker than at the bottom. This means that it is closer to the viewer, compensating for its greater height above the ground. From a distance, this device cannot be detected, but it makes the panels much easier to see. However, the Parthenon's artists also used techniques we would find surprising today. They used wax and pigments to paint their carvings in brilliant colors. And they fixed metal trimmings on sandals, bridles and armor.

keep clear of the wheels and the horses' flying hooves. This display had originally formed part of the army's training. But Athenian soldiers no longer used chariots in war. Their most powerful weapon in the 5th century BC was their well-armed fleet. Now the skills of the apobatai were preserved just for display during the Great Panathenaic procession.

people are shown on the frieze; we see mostly young men and horses. There are few of the the foot-soldiers who usually took part. At (3) girls carry unidentified square objects. Archaeologists have suggested that they are stone tablets recording the city's spending on the festival – everything was paid for by the state, or by wealthy citizens and officials. Historians have also suggested that the tablets might contain lists of dead heroes' names.

Charioteer

Apobates (soldier)

Four horses pulling chariot

OFFERINGS FOR ATHENA

The East Frieze begins and ends with groups of girls carrying items to be used in the sacrifice. In (1) they are carrying bowls and one jugs; in (9) a girl carries an incense burner. Then the festival organizers are shown (2). Twelve gods and goddesses (3 and 7) are portrayed as seated figures, arranged in two groups on either side of the central human scene. To show their greatness, the gods are carved larger than life size.

The religious climax of the Panathenaic festival came when the new peplos was offered to the goddess. As the Athenians draped their offering over Athena's statue, they hoped that she and the other gods would see their actions and be pleased with the gift. The sculptors of the Parthenon have tried to illustrate this 'meeting' with Athena and the other, invisible, gods in their carvings along the East Frieze.

The birthday offering was followed by slaughter, other sacrifices and prayers at the ancient altar of Athena, where her first temple had stood. Sacrifices were not made at the Parthenon itself. There were no altars inside or outside the building. The great statue of Athena was offering enough.

Although most citizens could not take part in the great procession, or in the sacrifices held on the Acropolis, they could still join in the celebrations to honor their goddess Athena. After the sacrifices, left-over meat was carried back into the city-state where it was distributed among citizens gathered in the Kerameikos quarter, waiting to receive their share of the feast. Tourists attending the festival brought little statues of Athena or other favorite gods. These 'vulgar little objects' (as a later historian called them) were made by Athenian craftsmen, who sold them as souvenirs.

The central panel shows two women (4) carrying footstools on their heads, greeted by a tall priestess (5). The stools were placed beside the altar, to invite the invisible goddess to sit

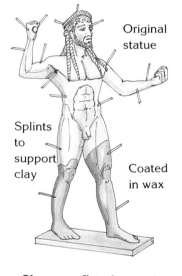

Original statue

Splints to support clay

Coated in wax

Clay was fitted over the wax-coated original, and left to set hard. The whole block was heated; the wax melted and was allowed to run away.

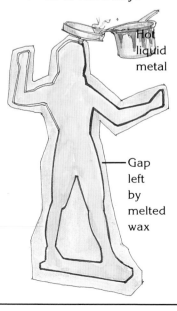

Hot liquid metal

Gap left by melted wax

Souvenir statues used the 'lost wax' process. A wooden carving was coated with wax.

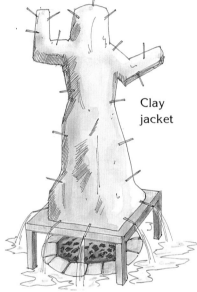

Clay jacket

Liquid metal was poured into the gap left between the wooden core and the clay, producing a hollow copy of the original.

Metal copy of original

Clay cover removed

3   4   5   6   7

and watch offerings being made. Then the chief priest of Athena receives the new peplos

(6) (carved less than life size); by the 5th century BC, the peplos was as large as a ship's sail. The

Ergastinai – girls from noble families who had woven the peplos for Athena that year – are

shown at (8). It was a great honor to be chosen for this task, which took 9 months.

8   9

Athenians rest after the festival procession and enjoy a feast of roast meat from the sacrificial animals, bread and wine.

PAST AND PRESENT

By the 3rd century BC, Athens was in decline. New and more powerful states, in Macedonia (northern Greece) and Rome, took control of the Mediterranean lands. The Parthenon became a tourist attraction, rather than the heart of a confident city-state.

In AD 330, Rome's territories were divided, and Athens became part of the Byzantine kingdom, centered in Constantinople. In 1456, Athens was captured by Muslim forces. Christians and Muslims both made alterations to the Parthenon, but its basic structure was unharmed. Disastrous damage occurred in 1687, when it was accidentally blown up.

Roman tourists (above) visited Greece to admire its many great buildings and works of art.

The Acropolis (below) in the 17th century. The Parthenon had become a Muslim mosque.

During the Middle Ages the Parthenon was converted into a Christian church.

It was dedicated to the Virgin Mary. She was honored as 'Our Lady of Athens'.

The Turks conquered Athens in the 15th century. In 1687, they were attacked by troops from Venice.

A Venetian cannonball hit the Parthenon, which was used to store gunpowder. The whole building exploded.

British and French people visited Greece during the 18th century as part of the fashionable 'Grand Tour' – a holiday spent studying art and fine buildings. The educated tourists were shocked by the condition of the Parthenon, shown here in 1776. A mosque had been built among the ruins, and there were poor houses all around.

Thomas Bruce (below), Lord Elgin (1766-1841). Right: Removing the remaining metopes from the Parthenon, 1801.

The civilization of ancient Greece was widely admired in 17th- and 18th-century Europe. Travelers felt they must rescue what was left of the Parthenon. One visitor, Lord Elgin, took action. He was British ambassador to the Turks, and persuaded the Turkish ruler of Athens to let him take many Parthenon sculptures back to England for safe keeping. This was arranged, and the 'Elgin Marbles', as they were known, were bought for Britain in 1816. Greece became independent in 1833, and started an intensive program of archaeological conservation. Today, many people feel that the Parthenon's sculptures should be returned to their original home.

Below **Drawings** of the Parthenon were lost when Elgin's ship *Mentor* sank in 1804.

Parthenon statues in the British Museum fascinated many 19th-century artists. Most of them felt that these great works were better than more 'modern' sculptures.

The Parthenon continues to attract tourists; millions visit it every year.

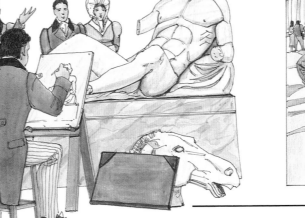

GREEK INFLUENCE

Greek temple architecture developed from simple beginnings to a magnificent style, full of elegance, proportion and grace. It is not surprising that it has been widely copied in buildings all around the world. There was only one period, the later Middle Ages (about 1100-1400 AD), when Greek temple designs were ignored. Then, builders and sculptors preferred the soaring Gothic style. (You can see examples of this in medieval cathedrals, and in some later buildings, too.) But scholars and architects of the Renaissance, which began in Italy in the 15th century, enthusiastically reintroduced classical Greek designs.

Greek ideas about temple architecture spread throughout the ancient world. They were even copied by enemies. This temple, which formed part of a theater complex, was built in the hostile Turkish city of Pergamon in the 2nd century BC. At that time, Athens' political power was weakening, but its cultural influence was still strong.

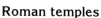

Roman temples developed directly from Greek designs. This temple, known as the 'Maison Carrée' (the Square House), was built in the Roman city of Nîmes, in France, around 15 BC. It has many Greek features.

Above
The Villa Rotonda (the Round House), designed by the Italian architect Palladio in 1567.

Below
Monticello, a country house in Virginia designed by Thomas Jefferson in 1767.

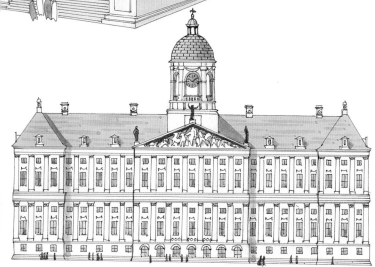

Amsterdam Town Hall (above),1648. Heveningham Hall Suffolk, (right), 1779.

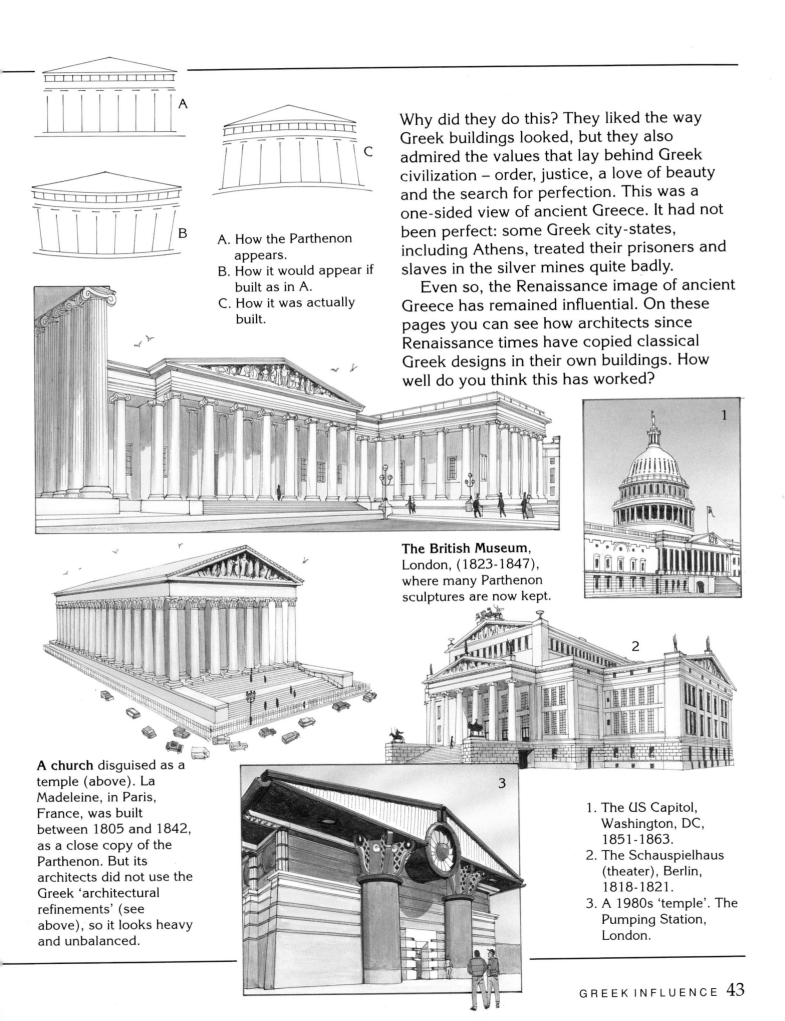

A. How the Parthenon appears.
B. How it would appear if built as in A.
C. How it was actually built.

Why did they do this? They liked the way Greek buildings looked, but they also admired the values that lay behind Greek civilization – order, justice, a love of beauty and the search for perfection. This was a one-sided view of ancient Greece. It had not been perfect: some Greek city-states, including Athens, treated their prisoners and slaves in the silver mines quite badly.

Even so, the Renaissance image of ancient Greece has remained influential. On these pages you can see how architects since Renaissance times have copied classical Greek designs in their own buildings. How well do you think this has worked?

The British Museum, London, (1823-1847), where many Parthenon sculptures are now kept.

A church disguised as a temple (above). La Madeleine, in Paris, France, was built between 1805 and 1842, as a close copy of the Parthenon. But its architects did not use the Greek 'architectural refinements' (see above), so it looks heavy and unbalanced.

1. The US Capitol, Washington, DC, 1851-1863.
2. The Schauspielhaus (theater), Berlin, 1818-1821.
3. A 1980s 'temple'. The Pumping Station, London.

TEMPLE FACTS

In 1842, Greek archaeologists started to rebuild the Parthenon. But they did not take as much care as the original builders had done. The iron clamps that they used to join the marble blocks are rusting away. As this happens, they expand, and crack the stone. Where possible, they are being replaced by bars of stainless steel and bronze.

Millions of tourists still visit the Parthenon. But their feet are wearing gulleys in the Acropolis, and most of the hill is fenced off.

The Parthenon has changed color, for two reasons. First, the marble has turned from white to yellow, caused by chemical reactions involving tiny particles of iron within the stone. Second, the bright colors used to 'paint' the Parthenon's sculptures have also worn away.

Building work on the Parthenon was controlled by the Athenian Assembly, which appointed overseers to make sure the city-state's money was being well spent. The overseers drew up careful accounts, which were carved on tablets of stone. Some of these tablets have survived until today.

Most of the Parthenon's sculptures are in museums, to preserve them from decay. The last three statues on the West Pediment were removed in 1976.

Pheidias, the sculptor, left Athens in disgrace after the scandal over his self-portrait on Athena's shield. (This is described on page 28.) He was also accused of stealing the gold used in Athena's statue. The gold panels were removed from the statue and weighed. Pheidias was proved innocent, but this quarrel soured his friendship with the city-state. He moved to the temple at Olympia, where he built another magnificent gold and ivory statue, this time of the god Zeus.

Itkinos and Kallicrates, the architects of the Parthenon, went on to build other famous temples, in Athens and elsewhere. Kallikrates designed the Temple of Nike in Athens, and Itkinos built the Temple of Apollo at Bassai.

Today, air pollution in Athens, caused by traffic fumes and acid rain, is gradually eating away at the Parthenon. Marble will dissolve in acid, and so the fine surface, produced by the 5th century sculptors, has suffered severe damage. Recently, it has been suggested that the Parthenon's columns should be injected with a special 'plastic' solution to hold the crumbling structure together. But some archaeologists are not sure whether this will work. Once injected, the bonding solution cannot be removed.

Myths of Athena

Myths and legends may not be true, but they can tell us what was important to people living long ago.

Food and water are among the most vital requirements of any civilization. One famous myth about Athena reflects these needs. The god Poseidon challenged Athena over who had the right to protect the city-state of Athens. He struck the Acropolis with his trident, and a spring of salt water gushed forth. This was impressive, but undrinkable. The wise Athena caused an olive tree to grow. It provided the citizens with seedlings, and ensured a steady supply of a useful, valuable commodity. Not surprisingly, Athena won the contest.

Another ancient myth, depicted on an early temple dedicated to Athena and built on the Acropolis, showed how she fought a brave and daring battle against invading giants. These monsters, like the centaurs shown on the metopes of the Parthenon, symbolized savagery and disorder. The Athenians felt they had no place in a civilized community. Like the myth of Athena's miraculous birth, springing fully-armed from the brain of her father Zeus (seen on the East Pediment of the Parthenon), they portrayed Athena as a goddess full of wisdom, energy and power.

Many Athenian citizens made their living as craftworkers. Men dug clay, shaped it into pots, and painted them with elegant designs in red and black. Athenian pottery was famous all over Greece, and is still admired today. As the city's favorite goddess, Athena shared in the potters' skills. Legends claimed that she had invented the potter's wheel, and had also designed the first Athenian vases.

Athenian women were famous for their weaving and embroidery. Athena, too, was skilful at craftwork. Among all of the goddesses, she was chosen to embroider the veil worn by Hera, Queen of the Heavens, wife of the supreme Greek god, Zeus.

Athena was jealous of her skills. She wanted to be recognized as the best weaver in the whole world. But one young girl called Arachne boasted that she was just as clever and skillful as Athena. Arachne wove a beautiful robe showing scenes from the lives of the gods and goddesses. Athena visited her home to inspect the work. She was furious to discover that it was, indeed, perfect, and as good as anything she could make. In her anger, Athena changed poor Arachne into a spider, condemned to spend her whole life spinning thread and weaving webs. To biologists, spiders are still known as 'arachnids' (a Greek word meaning 'children of Arachne') today.

GLOSSARY

Acroteria (singular: Acroterion), carved decorations at the three 'corners' of each pediment.

Agonothetai, festival organizers.

Anathyrosis, the smooth 'frame' carved at the ends of blocks of stone, designed to ensure a close fit.

Antefixes (singular: Antefix), ornaments fixed at regular intervals along the long sides of a roof.

Apobates (plural: Apobatai), a young soldier who jumped on and off moving chariots.

Archaeology, the study of the past from physical remains.

Architectural refinement, a device, or 'trick', designed to make a building look right.

Architrave, a beam (of wood or stone) resting on the tops of two or more columns.

Battens, thin strips of wood.

Bung, stopper or plug.

Buttress, strong support.

Cantering, a horse moving at a pace faster than a trot but slower than a gallop.

Cavalry, soldiers who fight on horseback.

Chiseled, cut with a sharp metal tool.

Chryselephantine, made from gold and ivory.

Cistern, pool or hollow chamber.

Classical, based on order and tradition. Usually a term of praise.

Column, a tall, circular pillar, made of stone.

Cornice, the 'trim' along the top of a frieze or a pediment.

Dedicated, given to a god.

Destiny, fate.

Drachma, a small silver coin, equaling a day's pay for a skilled worker.

Dramatist, someone who writes plays.

Doric, the plain, solid, simple style of architecture common in southern and western Greece.

Entrails, heart, lungs, liver and intestines.

Ergastinai, young girls who wove Athena's peplos.

Flutes, (1) musical instruments or (2) thin grooves cut all the way down columns.

Frieze, a horizontal band of decoration running around a building, resting on top of the architrave.

Gothic, a movement in European arts that developed in the 12th century and lasted throughout the Middle Ages. Gothic architecture is characterized by pointed arches, high spires, intricate stonework, and extensive use of stained glass and sculpture.

Great Panathenaia, an extra-special version of the Panathenaic festival, held once every four years.

Honeycomb, a soft, waxy 'framework' of cells, each filled with honey. Made by bees.

Hoplites, foot-soldiers in ancient Greece.

Humidity, dampness.

Illusion, pretence.

Intellectual, someone interested in ideas.

Ionic, the graceful, decorated and sometimes elaborate style of architecture common in eastern Greece and Asia Minor (modern Turkey).

Javelin, a weapon like a spear.

Kithara, a musical instrument, like a small harp.

Marble, a smooth, crystalline stone, used mainly for sculpture. The Parthenon is built of marble.

Metics, foreigners who lived in Athens.

Metope, a stone panel, placed above an architrave like a frieze. Metopes were fixed alternately with triglyphs.

Mounts, animals that are ridden.

Mules, the offspring of a male donkey and a female horse.

Naos, inner room.

Oracle, a sacred place where people could ask the gods questions about problems. The word can also refer to the priestess who spoke for the god and the messages given by the priestess. Her mysterious messages were interpreted by priests.

Panathenaia, an Athenian festival, held every year in honor of their patron goddess Athena.

Parian, from the Greek island of Paros.

Pediment, the triangular panel at each end of a temple roof.

Peplos, long robe worn by Greek women. The Athenians presented a new peplos to Athena every year.

Peripteral, built to include a peristyle.

Peristyle, a covered row of columns surrounding all four sides of a temple.

Pigment, a stain or a dye. Greek pigments were often made of finely-crushed stone.

Polis, the Greek word for town or city.

Pronaos, porch.

Proportions, the relationship of all the different parts of one whole.

Renaissance, an artistic and intellectual movement in 15th and 16th century Europe, when ancient Greek and Roman ideas became fashionable.

Sacrifices, offerings to the gods.

Severed, cut off.

Stylobate, the top step of a temple base.

Talent, a large sum of money, equal to over 16 years' pay for a skilled worker.

Triglyph, panels, usually carved in grooves to look like wood, placed in between each metope.

Translucent, allowing a little light to shine through.

Volutes, the spiral shapes used to decorate the tops of Ionic columns.

INDEX